Hotel for Dogs

by Lois Duncan

Lit Link
Grades 4-6

Written by Nat Reed
Illustrated by S&S Learning Materials

About the author:
Nat Reed has been a member of the teaching profession for over 30 years. He is presently a full-time instructor at Trent University in the Teacher Education Program.

ISBN: 978-1-55495-062-1
Copyright 2010
All Rights Reserved * Printed in Canada

Published in the U.S.A by:
On The Mark Press
P.O. Box 433
Clayton, New York
13624
www.onthemarkpress.com

Published in Canada by:
S&S Learning Materials
15 Dairy Avenue
Napanee, Ontario
K7R 1M4
www.sslearning.com

Permission to Reproduce
Permission is granted to the individual teacher who purchases one copy of this book to reproduce the student activity material for use in his/her classroom only. Reproduction of these materials for an entire school or for a school system, or for other colleagues or for commercial sale is strictly prohibited. No part of this publication may be transmitted in any form or by any means, electronic, mechanical, recording or otherwise without the prior written permission of the publisher. "We acknowledge the financial support of the Government of Canada through the Book Publishing Industry Development Program (BPIDP) for this project."

At A Glance

Learning Expectations	Ch 1	Ch 2	Ch 3	Ch 4	Ch 5	Ch 6	Ch 7	Ch 8	Ch 9	Ch 10	Ch 11	Ch 12	Ch 13	Ch 14	Ch 15
Reading Comprehension															
• Identify and describe story elements	•	•	•	•	•	•	•	•	•	•	•	•	•	•	•
• Summarize events/details	•	•	•	•	•	•	•	•	•	•	•	•	•	•	•
• Character traits, comparisons	•		•	•	•			•		•	•	•			
• Use context clues	•	•	•	•	•	•	•	•	•	•	•	•	•	•	•
• Make inferences (why events occurred, characters' thoughts and feelings)	•	•	•	•	•	•	•	•	•	•	•	•	•	•	•
• Identify setting	•														
• Understand abstract concepts – conscience, revenge, fear, perseverance, self-respect, exaggeration, conflict, etc.	•	•			•	•	•	•	•				•	•	•
Reasoning & Critical Thinking Skills															
• Develop opinions and personal interpretations	•	•	•	•	•	•	•	•	•	•	•	•	•	•	•
• Write a letter						•									
• Conduct an interview										•					
• Identify/create a *simile*		•													
• Identify *cliffhanger*									•					•	
• Identify *onomatopoeia*												•			
• Identify/create an *alliteration*	•														
• Write a news article											•				
• Identify point of view														•	
• Identify *conflict*							•								
• Identify the *climax* of a story															•
• Develop a time line															•
• Complete book cover														•	
• Identify an *analogy*											•				
• Interpret an *expression* of speech					•				•			•			
• Create a storyboard													•		
• Create a poem		•													
• Practice research skills			•	•						•		•			
• Write a book review														•	
• Predict an outcome				•		•	•	•						•	•
Vocabulary Development, Grammar, & Word Usage															
• Identify synonyms, antonyms, and homonyms				•	•					•	•	•	•	•	
• Identify syllables		•													
• Identify parts of speech							•		•						
• Dictionary and thesaurus skills		•	•	•					•				•		•
• Use words correctly in sentences	•	•					•	•		•				•	
• Place words in alphabetical order				•											
• Identify compound words										•					
• Identify root words								•							
• Using capitals, correct punctuation					•										

Table of Contents

At A Glance™ 2

Overall Expectations 4

List of Skills 5

Teacher Suggestions 6

Synopsis/Author Biography 7

Student Checklist 8

Reproducible Student Booklet 9

Answer Key 60

Overall Expectations

The students will:

- develop their skills in reading, writing, listening, and oral communication.

- use good literature as a vehicle for developing skills required by curriculum expectations: reasoning and critical thinking, knowledge of language structure, vocabulary building, and use of conventions.

- become meaningfully engaged in the drama of literature through a variety of types of questions and activities.

- identify and describe elements of stories (i.e., plot, main idea, characters, setting).

- learn and review many skills in order to develop good reading habits.

- provide clear answers to questions and well-constructed explanations.

- organize and classify information to clarify thinking.

- learn about: bullying, adjusting to new and difficult circumstances, pet care, handling responsibilities, developing perseverance when facing difficult circumstances, the importance of cooperation and teamwork in a crisis, and character development/growth.

- relate events and the feelings of characters found in the novel to their own lives and experiences.

- learn the importance of dealing with adversity and developing perseverance in the face of difficult experiences.

- state their own interpretation of a written work, using evidence from the novel and from their own knowledge and experience.

List of Skills

Vocabulary Development:
1. Locating descriptive words/phrases
2. Listing synonyms & antonyms
3. Identifying/creating onomatopoeia
4. Use of capitals and punctuation
5. Identifying syllables
6. Listing compound words
7. Identifying/creating a simile
8. Use of singular/plural nouns
9. Using context clues: analogies
10. Identifying parts of speech
11. Determining alphabetical order
12. Identification of root word
13. Identifying/creating alliteration
14. Identifying examples of sarcasm

Setting Activities:
1. Summarize the details of a setting

Plot Activities:
1. Complete a time line of events
2. Identify conflict in the story
3. Identify the climax of a novel
4. Identify cliffhangers

Character Activities:
1. Determine character traits
2. Compare characters
3. Relating personal experiences
4. Identifying point of view

Art Activities:
1. Design a cover for the novel
2. Create a Storyboard
3. Sketch a picture
4. Create a book cover

Creative and Critical Thinking:
1. Research
2. Write a newspaper article
3. Write a letter to a friend
4. Compare the novel with the movie
5. Conduct an Interview
6. Write a description of your feelings
7. Create your own poem
8. Write a review of the novel

Teacher Suggestions

This resource can be used in a variety of ways:

1. The student booklet focuses on one chapter of the novel at a time. Each of these sections contains the following activities:

    a) **Before you read the chapters** (reasoning and critical thinking skills)
    b) **Vocabulary building** (dictionary and thesaurus skills)
    c) **Questions on the chapter** (reading comprehension skills)
    d) **Language activities** (grammar, punctuation, word structure, and extension activities)

2. Students may read the novel at their own speed and then select or be assigned, a variety of questions and activities.

3. **Bulletin Board and Interest Center Ideas:** dogs and other pets (especially Irish Setters, dachshunds), "bullying", New Jersey, photography; moving to a new home.

4. **Pre-Reading Activities:** *Hotel for Dogs* may also be used in conjunction with themes of the importance of cooperation when undertaking a large project; dealing with adversity; peer pressure and bullying; developing personal responsibility.

5. **Independent Reading Approach:** Students who are able to work independently may attempt to complete the assignments in a self-directed manner. Initially these students should participate in the pre-reading activities with the rest of the class. Students should familiarize themselves with the reproducible student booklet. Completed worksheets should be submitted so that the teacher can note how quickly and accurately the students are working. Students may be brought together periodically to discuss issues in specific sections of the novel.

6. **Fine Art Activities:** Students may integrate such topics as themes dealing with pets and pet care; breeds of dogs; collages; a Storyboard; book covers.

7. Encourage the students to keep a reading log in which they record their readings each day and their thoughts about the passage.

8. Students should keep all their work together in one place. A portfolio cover is provided for this reason.

9. Students should not be expected to complete all of the activities. Teachers should allow choices and in some cases match the activity to the student's ability.

10. Students should keep track (in their portfolio) of the activities they complete.

Hotel for Dogs
by Lois Duncan

Synopsis

Hotel For Dogs is the charming story of Andi and Bruce, who reluctantly move with their family from Albuquerque, New Mexico to Elmwood, New Jersey. The move to Elmwood has presented the family with a number of unique challenges, not the least of which is sharing a house with their great aunt, Alice, an elderly woman given to hypochondria. There they also meet a most unpleasant neighbor – Jerry, a rich snobby kid who terrorizes his pet Irish Rover, and has every kid in the neighborhood cowed into bowing to his every whim.

Through an interesting set of circumstances, Andi and Bruce soon find themselves guardians of a number of stray dogs which cross their paths. They decide to harbor them in a vacant house just down the street. One of these animals is Red Rover, Jerry's terrorized Irish Setter, who has run away from home.

Joined by a couple of like-minded friends, they soon find that tending to such a menagerie of animals is quite expensive, and requires a lot of work (including getting up very early to walk them).

When they decide to play a prank on Jerry to teach him a lesson about cruelty to animals, Andi and Bruce's world slowly comes crashing down. In the following repercussions, however, they discover an unexpected ally in Aunt Alice. Their fortunes turn for the better when their parents decide to buy the vacant house, and Jerry's dad gives Bruce the opportunity to purchase Red Rover. Although the hotel for dogs has come to an end, the experience has given both Andi and Bruce a place in the community, and a couple of good friends who will help them settle into their new home in the town of Elmwood, New Jersey.

Author Biography
Lois Duncan

Lois Duncan was born in Philadelphia, Pennsylvania but raised in Sarasota, Florida. Both of her parents were well-known photographers. Like Andi, the main character in Hotel For Dogs, Lois began writing at a very young age (10) and sold her first story when she was only 13. She briefly attended Duke University but dropped out to marry and start a family. Over the course of her writing career she saw more than 300 of her articles published as well as a number of novels. She is best known for writing novels of suspense for teenage readers. Her most famous is **I Know What You Did Last Summer**, which like **Hotel For Dogs**, was made into a movie. One of her most recent novels, **News For Dogs**, is a sequel to **Hotel For Dogs**. For a number of years Lois has taught journalism at the University of New Mexico, in Albuquerque, where she lives with her husband, Don Arquette. She has five children.

Student Checklist

Student Name: _____

Assignment	Grade/Level	Comments

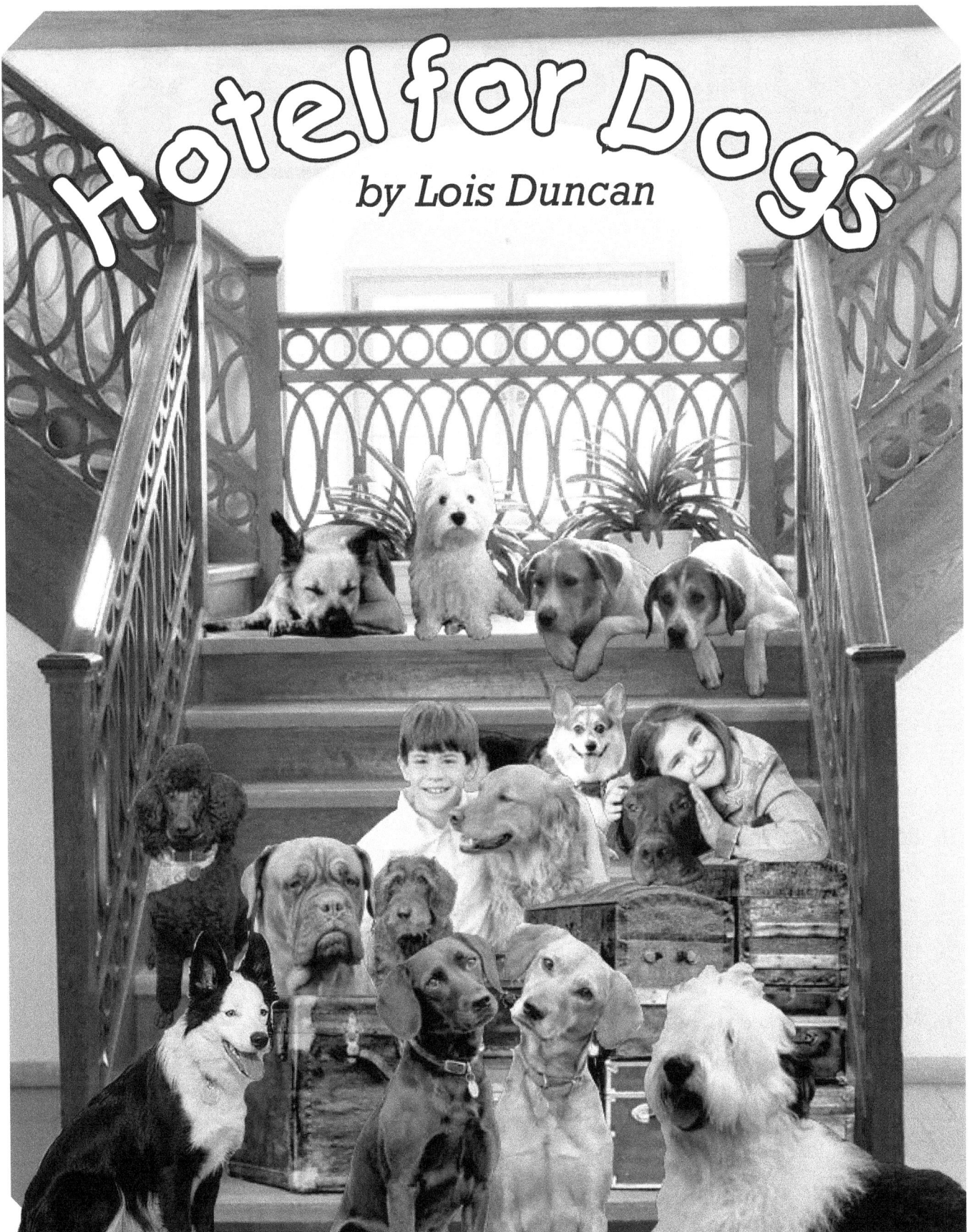

Name: _____

Chapter 1

Before you read the chapter:

Have you ever been required by your family or friends to make a **sacrifice** for the betterment of all concerned? How did making such a sacrifice make you feel?

_____
_____
_____
_____

Vocabulary:

Choose a word from the list to complete each sentence.

| simultaneously | sulk | pedigree | dorky | curtly |
| resent | skeptical | promotion | evidently | incredulous |

1. Both Jane and Thomas remained _____ about whether the salesperson was really telling the truth.

2. When I gave her my excuse, my aunt gave me a most _____ look.

3. If you're not careful, people will begin to _____ you bragging about your good fortune.

4. My mother worked very hard for several years before receiving her _____.

5. After not getting what she had asked for, my sister began to _____.

6. A dog with such a respected _____ is sure to be worth a lot.

7. The impatient police officer answered her most _____.

8. "Oh don't act so _____, Emily," she said. "People will think you're very immature."

9. The barn and the farm house were destroyed _____ by the hurricane.

10. _____ she doesn't like cats as much as dogs.

Hotel for Dogs
by Lois Duncan

Questions:

1. The **setting** of a story includes not only where but when the story takes place. What is the setting of Chapter One?

2. a) What was Andi's appraisal of Aunt Alice's house?

   b) What was the underlying reason for such a harsh appraisal?

3. What sacrifice did Andi make as a part of their move?

4. Why did the family have to move?

5. a) What was Aunt Alice's impression of Jerry?

   b) How did this conflict with Andi's impression?

c) What is your impression of Jerry? Support your answer with evidence from the novel.
_____
_____

6. You have already met a number of the key characters in this novel. In the chart below, list one important descriptor about each character (either appearance or personality).

Andi	
Bruce	
Aunt Alice	
Jerry	

Language Activity:

The author seems to enjoy using **alliteration** – a literary device where the author repeats the same consonant sound at the beginning of several words in close succession. An example from this chapter is: "**w**estern **w**eirdo" and "**s**weetest **s**mile."

Using your imagination, create your own examples of **alliteration** from the following topics. Each example must contain a minimum of three words.

The sound of a thunderstorm at night   _____

The cry of a hungry baby   _____

The squishy sound of quicksand   _____

In the box below, illustrate one of the alliterations that you created.

Chapter 2

Before you read the chapter:

In this chapter, Andi finds it difficult adjusting to her new school. Describe a time in your own life when you had to adjust to something new (i.e. a new home or school). How did you feel? What finally helped you to feel more at home in this new setting?

_____
_____
_____

Vocabulary:

Many of the following words are from Chapter Two. Use the words in the box to complete the following crossword puzzle.

Hotel for Dogs
by Lois Duncan

Down
1. Also known as a "wiener dog"
2. Blades on one's feet
3. Empty
4. Moved quickly
6. Fury; great anger
8. Midday meal
9. Victors
10. Not wet
14. ___ and fro
15. Rhymes with "bend"
16. An instrument owned by Bruce
19. ____ Elementary School
21. To form a mental image
24. Great fear
25. Eternal
26. _____ Gordon
28. Scolds
33. A porker

Across
5. Andi's surname
7. Aunt _____
11. Bruce's hobby
12. To convey or transport
13. Treasure _____
15. A part of the body
17. One less than two
18. Andi's dog
20. The novel's main character
22. Identical
23. In between two objects
27. Andi's brother
29. Lineage of a purebred animal
30. To the inside of
31. Destroyed
32. Answer
34. The Walkers were ____ of Aunt Alice

respond	endless	Bruce	into	champs	carry
dachshund	ruined	scurried	one	dry	Jerry
middle	camera	rage	to	pig	skates
Walker	Elmwood	vacant	Andi	Bebe	Alice
houseguests	chides	chest	lunch	send	dread
photography	stomach	pedigree	same	imagine	

Questions:

1. a) Describe the misunderstanding which resulted from the game Double Trouble.
   _____
   _____

b) Describe Andi's dilemma when she finally realized what Double Trouble actually was.

_____

_____

2. a) How long had Bebe been with Andi's family?

_____

b) Describe how Bebe became a part of the Walker family.

_____

_____

3. a) Andi is faced with another dilemma when she comes across the stray dog outside her aunt's house. Describe what happened.

_____

_____

b) What activity helped Andi to work out her feelings after the incident with the stray dog?

_____

_____

4. Andi says that if she reached the age of eleven without having had a poem published she would give up writing and turn to something else. Do you think this is wise? Defend your answer.

_____

_____

5. A *cliffhanger* is a literary device in which the chapter of a novel ends on a suspenseful note. How does Chapter Two end as a cliffhanger?

_____

_____

Hotel for Dogs
by Lois Duncan

Language Activities:

A. A *simile* is a comparison of two things using the words "like" or "as." An example of a simile from this chapter is: *... tail long and thin like a piece of black wire...*

What two things are being compared? _____ and _____

Invent your own simile comparing the following subject with something appropriate:

a) a piece of macaroni

_____
_____

B. Andi seems to enjoy writing poems. What was your impression of the poem she wrote in this chapter?

_____
_____

There are many forms of poetry. **A Quatrain**, for instance, is a poem consisting of four lines. Lines 2 and 4 must rhyme while having a similar number of syllables. Here is an example:

> *This morning on our trip to town*
> *We passed a big gas truck*
> *It was red and white and shiny*
> *'Till the moment it blew up.*

Now put on your thinking cap and write your own **Quatrain**. You may wish to choose a topic from **Hotel for Dogs** – such as dogs, moving to a new place/school, snobby rich kids, or stuffy aunts.

_____
_____
_____
_____

Chapter 3

Before you read the chapter:

Aunt Alice seems to be something of a *hypochondriac*. Investigate what this word means and then as you read Chapter Three, find proof for this contention to record below.

_____
_____

Vocabulary:

In each of the following sets of words, underline the one word that does not belong. Then write a sentence explaining why it does not fit.

1. resist   withstand   oppose   comply
_____

2. astonish   surprise   expect   flabbergast
_____

3. blessing   disaster   catastrophe   accident
_____

4. mistreat   coddle   abuse   brutalize
_____

5. reluctant   hesitant   averse   anxious
_____

6. tolerate   insist   assert   maintain
_____

7. confront   accost   avoid   face
   _____

8. systematic   orderly   precise   chaotic
   _____

9. unison   together   discord   alliance
   _____

10. eager   grudging   reluctant   resent
    _____

Questions:

Cloze Activity:

Complete the following exercise filling in the correct words from the **Word Box**.

den	sewing	Rover	friend	roast
Bruce	puppies	kitchen	dog	feathers
rubber	game	pool		

While the family was eating dinner, all Andi could think about was the smell of the _____ beef wafting through the house. She was worried that the hungry _____ upstairs would smell it. Aunt Alice told Andi's family that she was even allergic to bird _____. She said that even her pillows were made of foam _____. Aunt Alice told them that the basement in Jerry's house included a _____ room with a _____ table and big-screen TV. Bruce surprised the rest of the family by saying that he didn't want Jerry for a _____. He informed his parents that Red _____ was afraid of Jerry. Andi's

Hotel for Dogs
by Lois Duncan

parents were surprised when she volunteered to clean up in the _____. It was here that _____ caught her trying to smuggle a dish of roast beef upstairs. Andi took the food up to the stray dog while the rest of the family was in the _____ watching TV. After searching the entire upstairs, they finally found the stray dog in the _____ closet. There Andi also found three brown-and-white _____.

Language Activities:

A. Investigate:

Red Rover, Jerry's dog, is an **Irish (or red) setter**. Irish setters are gun dogs developed in Ireland in the 1700s. They are still popular today as hunting and family dogs and are renowned for their beauty.

Using resources from your school library or the Internet, research <u>three</u> interesting facts about this popular breed of dog.

_____
_____
_____
_____

B. Choose ten words from these chapters with two or more *syllables*. Indicate the syllables by drawing a line between each syllable. **Example: set/ter**

_____   _____
_____   _____
_____   _____
_____   _____
_____   _____

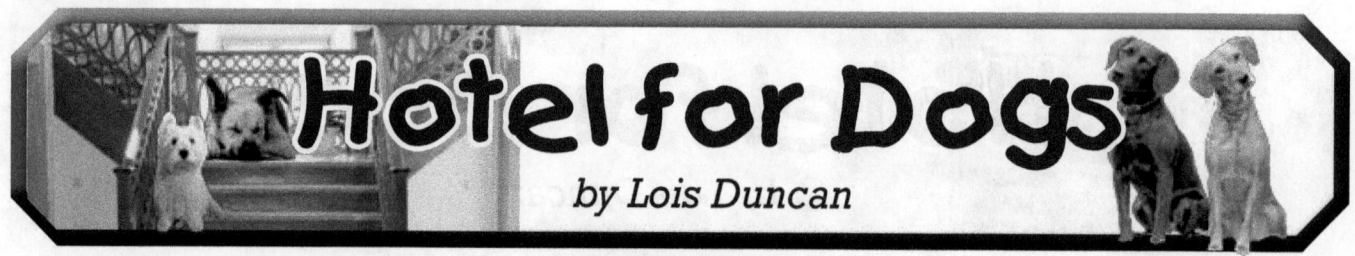

Chapter 4

Before you read the chapter:

Thomas Jefferson once said,

"In matters of style, swim with the current; In matters of principle, stand like a rock."

In their relationship with Jerry, we find that Andi and Bruce are both people who stick to their principles. Describe what is meant by this statement?

_____

_____

_____

Vocabulary:

Draw a straight line to connect the vocabulary word to its synonym. Remember to use a straight edge (like a ruler).

1. exasperation   a) assured
2. reasonable   b) thankful
3. confident   c) unhappy
4. concentrate   d) unbelieving
5. appreciate   e) annoyance
6. confrontation   f) horrified
7. miserable   g) concerned
8. incredulous   h) fair
9. appalled   i) conflict
10. sympathetic   j) contemplate

Questions:

1. Bruce gives a thoughtful analysis of his sister at the beginning of this chapter. In the chart below indicate Andi's good points and bad points (according to her brother, at least).

Good Points	Bad Points

2. Bruce and Andi are in a dilemma about what to do with the dogs at the beginning of the chapter. Andi asks, "What do you want to do, throw them out on the street?" Brainstorm with a partner for at least two alternative choices to *keeping them in the house or throwing them out on the street*.

   _____
   _____
   _____
   _____

3. What plan did Bruce finally come up with for the following day?

   _____
   _____

4. Describe how Jerry insulted Bruce when they were in class together.

   _____
   _____

5. What grade was Bruce in?

   _____
   _____

6. Why had the family, who had once lived down the street from Jerry, moved to another school district?
   _____
   _____

7. What evidence is there in the chapter that Bruce was a proud person?
   _____
   _____

8. Predict what you think Bruce has in mind for the abandoned building.
   _____
   _____

Language Activities:

A. Place the following words from this chapter in **alphabetical order**.

sometimes	1.
school	2.
statement	3.
seventh	4.
sale	5.
slowly	6.
standing	7.
seemed	8.
setting	9.
surrounding	10.

Hotel for Dogs
by Lois Duncan

B. Bruce certainly feels badly about the boy that Jerry picked on. Describe a similar emotional experience in your own life. What happened and how did you feel?

_____
_____
_____
_____

C. Write the plural form of the following nouns from this chapter. Careful – you may wish to consult a dictionary for some of these words.

Singular Noun	Plural Noun
family	
class	
puppy	
district	
activity	
hallway	
bush	
choice	
stomachache	
kindergarten	

Research Activity:

D. Albuquerque was the home of Andi and Bruce before moving to Aunt Alice's.

Using resources in your school library or on the Internet, research answers to the following questions about this important city.

What state is Albuquerque located in?	
What is the population of Albuquerque?	
What famous river does the city straddle?	

Chapter 5

Before you read the chapter:

Put the following quotation by *Harvey S. Firestone* into your own words, then state whether you agree or disagree with the quote and explain why:

> *Never be bullied into silence. Never allow yourself to be made a victim. Accept no one's definition of your life, but define yourself.*

_____
_____
_____
_____

Vocabulary:

Choose a word from the list that means the same or nearly the same as the underlined word.

adjust	interference	intent	cringe	appreciative
assault	decisive	tentative	bewildered	faucet

1. Mrs. Potter was quite **definite** about who was in her garden. _____
2. Martin appeared to be **confused** after the accident. _____
3. The only thing needing replacement will be the **spigot**. _____
4. Jackie seemed very **resolute** when she met me on the sidewalk. _____
5. The president was most **unwilling** to lead the country into war. _____
6. I saw the dog **cower** when Sammy raised his hand. _____
7. Her constant **meddling** will one day get her into big trouble. _____
8. The **attack** on the twins was very unexpected. _____
9. Were you able to **adapt** to the sudden climate change? _____
10. I was most **thankful** for having such wonderful friends. _____

Hotel for Dogs
by Lois Duncan

Questions:

1. What did Bruce plan on doing with the pups as soon as they were old enough?

2. Why do you think Bruce was nervous about letting the pups stay in the vacant house?

3. a) When Bruce was asked where Andi was, what proved to be most difficult for him?

   b) Why do you think this was the case?

4. Do you think it is ever right for someone to lie? Defend your answer.

5. Describe what resulted when Red Rover was hooked to the wagon.

6. What was Tim's reaction to this incident?

Hotel for Dogs
by Lois Duncan

Language Activities:

A. Comparing Bruce and Jerry

Despite having a few similarities, Bruce and Jerry are two very different characters. In the comparison framework below compare these two individuals by selecting criteria you feel reveals the similarities and/or differences between these two boys. You may select items regarding their appearance and/or character.

Criteria	Bruce	Jerry
1.		
2.		
3.		
4.		

B. Rewrite the following sentences putting in the **correct capitalization** and **punctuation**.

1. just this past tuesday jerry took red rover for a walk to burger king

   _____
   _____

2. when did you get to see the chicago bulls play

   _____
   _____

3. shania twain was raised in the town of timmins in northern canada

   _____
   _____

Hotel for Dogs
by Lois Duncan

Chapter 6

Before you read the chapter:

In Chapter 6 Bruce is faced with a dilemma. Define dilemma, then tell about a time when you faced one.

_____
_____
_____

Vocabulary:

Solve the following **word search puzzle** using the words from the Word Box. Remember – the words can be horizontal, vertical or diagonal. They may be forward or even backward!

stressful	dissolve	depression	anticipate	undignified
bureau	disgust	expression	conceal	gesture
defensive	frayed	miserable	tenant	grateful

```
F Q W E R N O I S S E R P X E
U R T Y U L U F E T A R G S L
N D A N T I C I P A T E T U B
D I A Y S D F G H J K R L N A
I S X C E V D B N M E Q W Z R
G G L K J D H I G S W E R T E
N U V B N O I S S E R P E D S
I S P O I U Y F T S R E W S I
F T L K J H U G F D O S A Z M
I M N N B L V C X Z Q L W E R
E P L A E C N O C O I U V Y T
D L K J N H G G E S T U R E G
M N D E F E N S I V E B V C X
M N B V C X T X Z U A E R U B
```

Questions:

1. How were Sundays different at Aunt Alice's compared to what Andi and Bruce were used to back in Albuquerque?

2. Do you think it is a good idea that Andi keeps all of her writings? Why or why not?

3. Why do you think Andi wasn't more upset about the way Jerry treated Red Rover when she and Bruce were discussing this together?

4. What did Bruce suggest was the only reason that Jerry might be upset at losing Red Rover?

5. What was Andi's motive for cleaning up after the meals for her mother and Aunt Alice?

6. Describe Red Rover's appearance when Andi and Bruce found him.

7. a) What did Bruce mean by his final statement in Chapter 6?

_____

_____

b) Predict how this might prove difficult.

_____

_____

Language Activity:

A. *A Letter Home*

Moving from Albuquerque to Aunt Alice's home proved to be difficult for Andi, her family, and especially for Aunt Alice. Put yourself in the position of one of the characters from the novel (i.e., Andi, Bruce, Aunt Alice) and compose a letter to a friend expressing your feelings about this new living situation. Be sure to include both the positives and negatives about the arrangement. Your letter should be at least a half-page in length and follow the proper format of a friendly letter.

B. Copy out any three sentences from this chapter and underline the ***verbs***.

_____

_____

_____

_____

_____

_____

_____

Chapter 7

Before you read the chapter:

In Chapter Seven Jerry's friend, Tim, makes an important decision that will change his life. Predict what you think this decision will involve. How do you think it will work out?

_____
_____
_____
_____
_____
_____

Vocabulary:

Write a sentence using the following words. Make sure that the meaning of the word is clear in your sentence.

evaluate: _____
_____

furious: _____
_____

incredulous: _____
_____

dictator: _____
_____

Hotel for Dogs
by Lois Duncan

loner: _____

exasperated: _____

luxurious: _____

transformation: _____

gesture: _____

triumphant: _____

Questions:

1. What did Andi accuse Tim of being at the beginning of this chapter? Why?

2. Why did Tim say he wouldn't have to be a loner if he wasn't a part of Jerry's gang?

Hotel for Dogs
by Lois Duncan

3. Why did the boys have to be careful when taking the boards to the vacant house?

   _____
   _____

4. Andi makes the statement, "At home Mom never minded if we let the dishes sit for a while before we loaded the dishwasher. Why should it matter so much here?" Why do you think it now mattered to Andi's mom?

   _____
   _____

5. Why do you think Andi took so much trouble to clean up the inside of the vacant house?

   _____
   _____

6. Bruce says about Aunt Alice, "I bet she's counting the days until she can have her house to herself again…" Put yourself in Aunt Alice's shoes and think of one positive thing about having Andi and her family stay with her, and one negative thing.

   _____
   _____

7. When Andi accuses Bruce of stealing Red Rover he defends his actions by saying, "I took Red for his own sake." Do you think Bruce was justified in taking Red Rover, or was taking the dog wrong? Defend your answer.

   _____
   _____

Language Activities:

A. Beside each of the following words from this chapter, write its **root word**.

1. furiously   _____
2. rinsed   _____
3. uncomfortable _____
4. activities   _____
5. certainty   _____
6. decidedly   _____
7. transformation _____
8. responsibility _____

B. We have already read about a number of important conflicts in this novel. **Conflict** is an important element in a novel. There are generally three types of conflict: **person against person**; **person against self**, and **person against nature**. Find three examples of conflict in *Hotel for Dogs*, and tell which type of conflict each is.

1. _____
   _____
   _____
   _____

2. _____
   _____
   _____
   _____

3. _____
   _____
   _____
   _____

Hotel for Dogs
by Lois Duncan

Chapter 8

Before you read the chapter:

In this chapter Andi receives a great disappointment. Tell about a time in your own life when you endured such an experience. Describe how it made you feel.

_____
_____
_____
_____

Vocabulary:

Choose a word from the list to complete each definition.

| ungracious | admiration | solemn | inconceivable | resent |
| irritable | infuriated | visualized | goriest | picky |

1. It is difficult not to _____ someone who is always criticizing you.

2. When her allergies are bothering her she becomes _____.

3. The museum guard was _____ when he saw the gum stuck to the dinosaur exhibit.

4. Andi felt that Aunt Alice was much too _____.

5. It is simply _____ that no one noticed the old man was missing.

6. That was definitely the _____ horror movie I have ever seen.

7. His _____ for the president knows no bounds.

8. The graduation ceremony was a _____ occasion.

9. Not to shake the principal's hand was very _____ of Samantha.

10. To keep from being nervous during my speech, I simply _____ everyone in the audience sitting in their underwear.

Hotel for Dogs
by Lois Duncan

Questions:

1. At the beginning of Chapter Eight, why did Andi resent Tim's involvement?

2. Tim and Bruce worked to earn money to buy things for the dogs. What did they buy with this money?

3. Andi's mother says to her, "Very few people are boring when you really get to know them." Do you agree with this statement? Defend your answer.

4. What was "encouraging" about the note that Andi received from *Ladies' Home Journal*?

5. Andi suggests a number of career possibilities for herself. In the chart below indicate why each of her suggestions was shot down by others in her family.

A helicopter pilot	
A ballet dancer	
A teacher	

6. Why wouldn't Debbie talk to others about her love of poetry?

   _____
   _____

7. Describe your impression of Andi's poem about shipwrecks.

   _____
   _____

8. Why did Andi finally decide to let Debbie in on the secret about the hotel for dogs?

   _____
   _____

Language Activity:

A. Find <u>three</u> examples of the following parts of speech from this chapter.

Nouns	Verbs	Adjectives
_____	_____	_____
_____	_____	_____
_____	_____	_____

Hotel for Dogs
by Lois Duncan

Chapter 9

Before you read the chapters:

"Getting in over your head" is an expression used to describe people who have taken on too much responsibility and have lived to regret it. In Chapter Nine, Bruce "gets in over his head." Describe a time in your own life, or the life of someone you know, when you "got in over your head."

_____
_____
_____
_____

Vocabulary:

Synonyms are words with similar meanings. Using the context of the sentences below, choose the best synonym for the underlined word in each sentence.

1. I can't believe that you would **contradict** me in front of our guests!
   a) corroborate   b) oppose   c) scold   d) tease

2. What did you say when she **volunteered**?
   a) rejoiced   b) skipped   c) complained   d) offered

3. That was certainly an odd **expression** that Mr. Tandy used.
   a) verbalization   b) habit   c) automobile   d) costume

4. I thought for sure that his reputation would be **enhanced** by today's events.
   a) destroyed   b) heightened   c) damaged   d) ignored

5. "What was your **expectation** regarding this position?" Mrs. Ryan asked.
   a) choice   b) salary   c) outlook   d) approval

6. Joanie got a sudden **wistful** look on her face.
   a) longing   b) angry   c) joyous   d) frightened

Hotel for Dogs
by Lois Duncan

7. Did you know that the area was **restricted**?
   a) citified   b) valuable   c) demolished   d) closed

8. Scotty was filled with **anticipation**.
   a) resignation   b) confusion   c) apprehension   d) delight

9. "I found the experience to be completely **exhilarating**," Aunt Alice informed them.
   a) exciting   b) boring   c) frightening   d) draining

10. "Please leave me alone," Nan said. "I must **concentrate**."
    a) read   b) sleep   c) think   d) disperse

Questions:

1. Describe MacTavish's reaction to being taken to the hotel for dogs.
   _____
   _____

2. Why did Tim and Bruce object so strenuously to MacTavish staying at the "hotel?"
   _____
   _____

3. Describe Bruce's dad's reaction to Bruce's report card.
   _____
   _____

4. Describe what happened the first time Bruce set his alarm clock for two hours earlier than he usually got up.
   _____
   _____

5. Why was it so hard on Bruce when he got up so early to walk Red Rover?
   _____
   _____

6. Describe what resulted when Bruce slept in and was late taking Red Rover for his walk.
   _____
   _____

7. Chapter 9 ends as a cliffhanger. Explain what a cliffhanger is, and why an author would use this literary device.
   _____
   _____

Language Activities:

A. *Interview* at least three other students for their views of this novel so far. (Try to get both positive and negative comments.) Write a brief *report* putting these views together.

   _____
   _____
   _____
   _____
   _____
   _____
   _____

Hotel for Dogs
by Lois Duncan

B. The author loves to use expressions in this novel. Put the following expressions from *Hotel For Dogs* in your own words.

Speaking about his sisters, Tim tells Bruce: *They'd catch me first and go tattling off to our parents.*	
grabbing his sister and shaking her until her teeth rattled	
Tim tells Bruce that Andi is *just acting like a girl*	

C. Try to reassemble the word parts listed below into 10 **compound words** found in this chapter.

play	our	house	door	noon	lids	door	after	up	time
thing	work	any	some	selves	times	out	bell	stairs	eye

1. _____
2. _____
3. _____
4. _____
5. _____
6. _____
7. _____
8. _____
9. _____
10. _____

Chapter 10

Before you read the chapter:

What breeds of dog do you think wouldn't have any trouble being adopted from a pet shelter? Why? What breeds do you think would have trouble? Why? Try to think of two or three examples of each.

_____
_____
_____
_____

Vocabulary:

Antonyms are words with opposite meanings. Draw a line from each word in Column A to its *antonym* in Column B. Then use the words in Column A to fill in the blanks in the sentences.

Column A	Column B
1. forlorn	prohibition
2. reasonable	apathetic
3. absolute	dismay
4. enthusiastic	plain
5. exotic	cheerful
6. delight	absurd
7. permission	limited

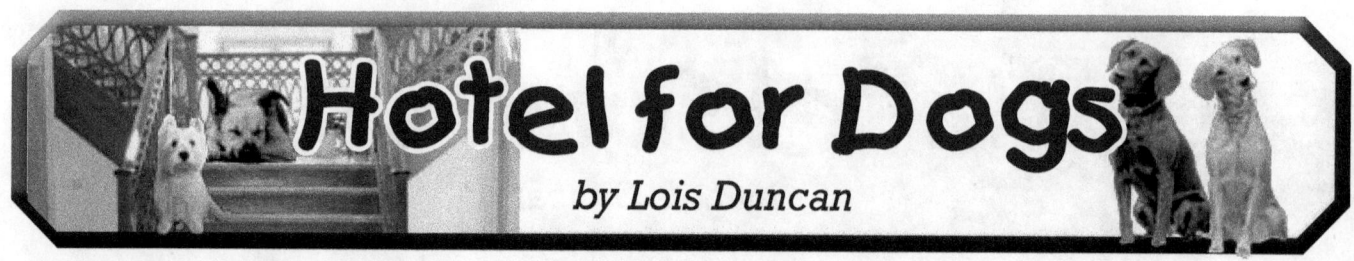

Hotel for Dogs
by Lois Duncan

1. Did you get your mother's _____ to attend the concert?

2. The cruel dictator had _____ authority over all the citizens of the island.

3. Is it _____ to expect everyone to do an honest day's work?

4. After the death of her cat I have never seen anyone looking as _____ as Katy did.

5. My little brother seemed most _____ about joining the floor hockey team.

6. The more _____ the parrot, the more costly it is.

7. "It is a real _____ for my wife and I to welcome you into our home," the warden said politely.

Questions:

Indicate whether the following statements are **True** or **False**.

1. Andi found herself resenting Red Rover so much that she wished they could send him away instead of the puppies. **T** or **F**

2. Andi's advertisement for the puppies was so small no one could read it. **T** or **F**

3. Tiffany Tinkle reminded Andi of a beige mouse. **T** or **F**

4. Tiffany's dog's puppies were part **Airedale** and part **Boxer**. **T** or **F**

5. Tiffany's dad planned on drowning the puppies if they could not find them a home soon. **T** or **F**

6. The vice principal stopped them from putting up an ad on the bulletin board. **T** or **F**

7. Andi's plans for Tiffany's puppies included eventually selling them to the circus. **T** or **F**

8. Debbie suggested that Tiffany tell her father that she had given the puppies to some classmates. **T** or **F**

9. Tiffany's puppies reminded the baby of Eeyore – the donkey from *Winnie the Pooh*. **T** or **F**

10. Chapter Ten ends with Jerry Gordon approaching the girls on the sidewalk. **T** or **F**

by Lois Duncan

Language Activities:

A. Chapter 10 introduces us to a rather interesting character – Tiffany – a girl who is quite different from Andi. **Compare** three things about these two girls. Consider such things as physical appearance, personality, age, talents, attitude, etc.

	Andi	Tiffany
1.		
2.		
3.		

B. Ginger's puppies certainly must have been very unusual in appearance, and even in personality. Using resources in your school library or the Internet, research three facts about either the Airedale or bulldog breed of dog. Then in the box below, sketch a picture of what you think Ginger's puppies might have looked like.

Breed:
1.
2.
3.

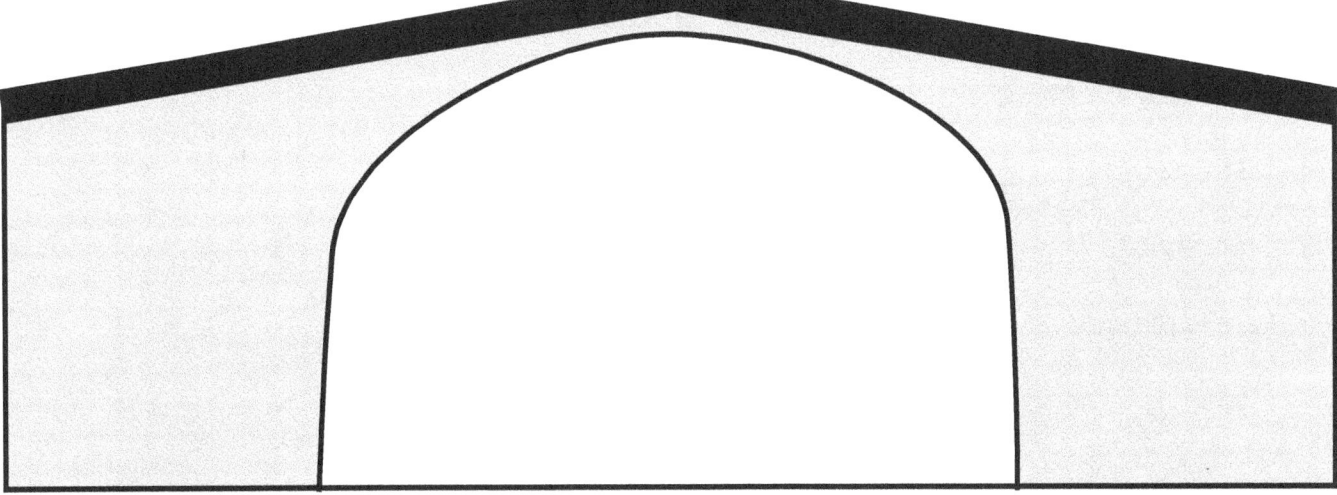

Chapter 11

Before you read the chapter:

In Chapter 11 Tiffany has a brainwave. What is a brainwave? Describe an example of a brainwave from your own experience.

_____
_____
_____
_____

Vocabulary:

Analogies are equations in which the first pair of words has the same relationship as the second pair of words. For example, **stop** is to **go** as **fast** is to **slow**. In this example, both pairs of words are opposites. Choose the best word from the word box to complete each of the analogies below.

irritable	torture	determination	frantic	intently
protective	skeptical	triumphant	confident	disbelief

1. Threatening is to _____ as hello is to goodbye.

2. Disbelieving is to _____ as courageous is to brave.

3. Distractedly is to _____ as soft is to rigid.

4. Distressed is to _____ as love is to adore.

5. Anguish is to _____ as superb is to exquisite.

6. Late is to tardy as victorious is to _____.

7. Modern is to ancient as cheerful is to _____.

Hotel for Dogs
by Lois Duncan

8. Intelligent is to smart as perseverance is to _____.

9. Smooth is to coarse as uncertain is to _____.

10. Tragic is to comic as trust is to _____.

Questions:

1. What was there about Jerry that surprised Andi when she saw him at the beginning of the chapter?

2. Describe how Andi almost said too much about Red Rover when speaking with Jerry.

3. What did Andi suggest the newspaper kid saw instead of Red Rover?

4. How did Tim confirm to Andi that what she had told Jerry was something that would bother him?

5. What two things did Andi say she would do instead of buying Christmas presents that year?

6. a) Describe Tiffany's brainwave.
   _____
   _____

   b) Can you think of any drawbacks to her plan?
   _____
   _____

Language Activity:

A. Imagine you are a writer for the local newspaper in the town in which Andi and Bruce are now living. You hear about the famous ghost dog seen by the local newspaper boy. Write a short article for your newspaper detailing the story. You may wish to interview Andi to get her unique ideas as well. Make sure you also describe your own opinions regarding this incident.

_____
_____
_____
_____
_____
_____
_____
_____
_____
_____

Chapter 12

Before you read the chapter:

There is an old expression heard sometimes which says, "things got out of hand". What does this expression mean, and how might it apply to our story at this point?

_____
_____
_____

Vocabulary:

Replace each word that is underlined in the sentences below with a word from the Word Box. Remember to consider the context of the word in the sentences, as some words have several meanings.

| impression | intently | astonishment | prelude | desperately |
| accommodations | obvious | insist | regretful | alterations |

1. It was very **plain** to everyone that she was fibbing. _____

2. The **prologue** to the event consisted of a banjo solo. _____

3. His **lodgings** for the summer were not fit for a dog to live in. _____

4. "I simply must **demand** that all of you leave!" his mother said in a loud voice. _____

5. He was most **apologetic** for the mistake. _____

6. What **impact** did your father have on your upbringing? _____

7. Most of the audience gazed in **amazement** at the magician. _____

Hotel for Dogs
by Lois Duncan

8. What **changes** in the garment do you recommend? _____

9. John was looking **fixedly** into the face of Sarah. _____

10. The collie dog was digging **frantically** at the base of the fence. _____

Questions:

1. a) What breed of dog was Preston?
   _____
   _____

   b) Describe his personality.
   _____
   _____

2. Why weren't Andi and her friends able to cut through the yard of the yellow house?
   _____
   _____

3. a) How did Aunt Alice react to the news that Andi's family might soon be moving from her house?
   _____
   _____

   b) Why was this a shock to Andi?
   _____
   _____

4. a) Describe how Preston disturbed the neighborhood. Why was this such a bad thing for Andi and the others?

_____

_____

b) How did Andi explain Preston's actions to Jerry? Do you think he bought her explanation? Explain your answer.

_____

_____

Language Activities:

A. *Investigation*

In this Chapter we meet another breed of dog – **the beagle**. Using resources in your school library or on the Internet, do an investigation of this amazing little breed of dog. Discover three interesting facts about the beagle and record your findings below

_____

_____

_____

_____

B. The author, Lois Duncan, enjoys using a variety of literary devices in this novel. One such device is ***onomatopoeia***. An example is "I'm going to – going to – going to – atchooooo!" Define ***onomatopoeia***, and use your imagination to think of another example of this device.

_____

_____

_____

_____

Chapter 13

Before you read the chapter:

When we are anxiously waiting for an event to happen it sometimes feels that it will never arrive. Describe a time in your life when time seemed to stand still.

_____
_____
_____

Vocabulary:

Think of synonyms for the following words. Use a thesaurus if necessary.

1. slumber _____

2. hasty _____

3. suppress _____

4. loomed _____

5. agony _____

6. dismay _____

7. frantic _____

8. illuminate _____

Questions:

1. The introduction to Chapter 13 has a distinctive mysterious atmosphere. How does the author accomplish this?

2. Investigate the meaning of the following items:

a) adobe	
b) tumbleweeds	
c) arroyos	
d) aspens	

3. During the slide presentation, which picture made Andi feel a great homesickness?

4. Who did Andi have for a sleep-over?

5. Describe the prank that Bruce and the others played on Jerry.

6. Describe how things did not end up going according to their plans.

Hotel for Dogs
by Lois Duncan

Extension Activity:

Storyboard:

A storyboard is a series of pictures that tell about an important event in a story. A storyboard can tell the story of only one scene – or the entire novel.

Complete the storyboard below illustrating the events described in Chapter 13. You may wish to practice your drawings on a separate piece of paper.

1.	2.
3.	4.
5.	6.

Chapter 14

Before you read the chapter:

After what happened at the end of the last chapter, predict what you think will happen next.
_____
_____
_____
_____

Vocabulary:

Choose a word from the list to complete each sentence.

| precise | convenient | wretched | bewilder | depressed |
| confident | queasy | melodious | grim | traditional |

1. After riding on the roller coaster, Betsy had a _____ feeling in her stomach.

2. The salesman had a _____ manner when dealing with the public.

3. No wonder you are feeling _____. It's not everyday that someone loses an aunt.

4. Mr. Knells, the town undertaker, is a very _____ person.

5. "I would rather we enjoy a more _____ celebration of the holiday," my grandmother said.

6. I am not sure what the _____ meaning of the word is.

7. Arriving just when we were serving dessert was a most _____ occurrence.

8. I didn't expect that the new software program would _____ him as it did.

Hotel for Dogs
by Lois Duncan

9. The accompanying tune written by my sister was much more _____ than the old one.

10. After suffering with influenza for almost a week, Mr. Hardy was feeling very _____.

Questions:

1. Why did Bruce say, "Everything's too quiet. It's like the stillness before a thunderstorm?"
   _____
   _____

2. Why was Bruce confident that they would be caught for the prank they had played on Jerry?
   _____
   _____

3. Why had Mr. Crabtree visited their home?
   _____
   _____

4. Whose house did Mr. Crabtree suggest they visit? Why?
   _____
   _____

5. Describe what resulted from their visit?
   _____
   _____
   _____
   _____
   _____

6. What did Mr. Crabtree propose they do about the dogs found in the empty house?

7. How did Chapter 14 end as a cliffhanger?

Language/Extension Activities:

A. *Sarcasm*, or *satire*, is a device used by the author in this chapter. For instance, when Bruce says, "Do you think Dad's not going to notice that? Especially when the cord's torn out of it and a matching cord has turned up in the Gordons' wall?" Look up the meaning of sarcasm and then using your imagination create an example of sarcasm.

B. Create a **book cover** for *Hotel for Dogs*. Be sure to include the title, author, and a picture that will make other students want to read the novel.

C. The author writes *Hotel for Dogs* as an **omniscient third person narrator** (as compared to the first person). An omniscient narrator is able to witness all the events of the story, and not just the ones that happen to the main character. He/she is also able to read the thoughts of all the characters and knows everything that has happened in the past to all of the characters. How would this point of view be an advantage in the telling of this story? How might it have been more interesting if it had been told from only Andi's point of view?

Chapter 15

Before you read the chapter:

Chapter 15 concludes this exciting novel. Describe how you think the author should end this novel in a way that you would find most satisfying.

_____
_____
_____
_____

Vocabulary:

Circle the correct word that matches the meaning of the underlined word.

1. My father **assembled** a team of experts to work on the project.

   a) hired   b) gathered   c) fired   d) blessed

2. Jasmine looked very **forlorn** while sitting on the porch.

   a) doubtful   b) embarrassed   c) carefree   d) lonely

3. Aunt Marjory's worn features had a most **placid** expression during much of our visit.

   a) calm   b) unhappy   c) tortured   d) serious

4. I don't really think his actions were **justified**.

   a) serious   b) legal   c) warranted   d) proved

5. Principal Skinner has very little **sympathy** for you today.

   a) compassion   b) time   c) indifference   d) hostility

6. "What did you say, Sir?" he asked **incredulously**.

   a) disappointedly   b) trustingly   c) excitedly   d) unbelieving

Hotel for Dogs
by Lois Duncan

7. My dad was very **skeptical** regarding John the Hired Man.

   a) trusting　　　b) doubtful　　　c) comforted　　　d) enraged

8. After a great deal of arguing, Matilda **submitted** to her aunt's will.

   a) ignored　　　b) disobeyed　　　c) complied　　　d) resisted

Questions:

1. Describe how Mr. Gordon reacted to the news that his son had knocked out all of the windows in the vacant house.

   _____
   _____

2. a) Describe Mr. Crabtree's initial reaction to the fact that Andi and the others had turned the house into a hotel for dogs? What did he feel should be the consequences for their behavior?

   _____
   _____

   b) What made him change his mind?

   _____
   _____

3. What astonishing piece of news did they learn about Aunt Alice in this chapter?

   _____
   _____

4. How did Mr. Gordon propose that Bruce purchase Red Rover. Why did he decide to sell the Irish Setter?

   _____
   _____

5. The climax of a story occurs when the main problem of the story is solved. Describe the event in this novel when the climax occurs.

_____
_____

6. Describe your own reaction to this novel's conclusion. Did it leave you feeling satisfied?

_____
_____

Language/Extension Activities:

A. A Time Line

Create a *time line* for *Hotel For Dogs* below, indicating the six most important events of the novel and the order in which they happened.

_____

_____

B. The Movie

Hotel For Dogs was released in 2009 as an exciting movie starring Emma Roberts. Lisa Kudrow of the television program, Friends, also appears in the movie. If you have a chance to watch the movie make a list of five things which differed from the novel, and <u>one</u> thing you liked more about either the novel or the movie.

C. A Book Review

Now is your chance to share your reactions to the novel with others. Write a review of the book, describing in no more than one paragraph an outline of the plot, and then in another paragraph how you enjoyed the novel (or didn't) and why. (Please don't give away the ending!)

This review can be posted to a website like www.amazon.com for others to enjoy.

Answer Key

Chapter 1 *(Page 10)*

Vocabulary:

1. skeptical 2. incredulous 3. resent 4. promotion 5. sulk
6. pedigree 7. curtly 8. dorky 9. simultaneously 10. evidently

Questions:

1. The story is set in Elmwood, New Jersey in recent times.
2. a) She thought it looked smug; stuck-up; too good for ordinary people. Even the grass looked fake.
   b) She resented having to leave their old home in New Mexico, and her dog Bebe.
3. Their dog, Bebe, was left with the Arquettes until Andi's family got a place of their own.
4. Andi's father had received a big promotion and was going to Elmwood for a training program.
5. a) Jerry was very popular. There's always a group of boys playing there. He was the sweetest boy.
   b) Andi thought he was rude and treated his dog cruelly.
   c) *Answers may vary.*
6. *Answers may vary.*

Chapter 2 *(Page 13)*

Vocabulary:

(Crossword puzzle with answers including: WALKED, ALICE, PHOTOGRAPHY, CARRY, CHESTOMACH, ONE, SAME, BED, AND, MIDDLE, JEDIGREE, BRUCE, INTO, RUINED, RESPOND, HOUSEGUESTS)

Questions:

1. a) Andi was asked to play the skipping game, Double Trouble, but she had never heard of the game so said "no." As a result the other girls thought she was a snob.
   b) When she realized what it was she wanted to play, but she didn't have the nerve to tell the other girls.
2. a) Almost three years.
   b) She had been under the Christmas tree all wrapped with Christmas paper.
3. a) She found a dog sitting on the porch steps. Andi brought it in to feed, but her mother made her take it back out. Then when no one was looking, Andi saw the dog sneak back into the house.

b) Writing a poem.
4. *Answers may vary.*
5. Andi sees the stray dog sneak into the house and head up the stairs.

Chapter 3 *(Page 17)*
Vocabulary:

1. comply	2. expect	3. blessing	4. coddle	5. anxious
6. tolerate	7. avoid	8. chaotic	9. discord	10. eager

Questions:

   While the family was eating dinner, all Andi could think about was the smell of the **roast** beef wafting through the house. She was worried that the hungry **dog** upstairs would smell it. Aunt Alice told Andi's family that she was even allergic to bird **feathers**. She said that even her pillows were made of foam **rubber**. Aunt Alice told them that the basement in Jerry's house included a **game** room with a **pool** table and big-screen TV. Bruce surprised the rest of the family by saying that he didn't want Jerry for a **friend**. He informed his parents that Red **Rover** was afraid of Jerry. Andi's parents were surprised when she volunteered to clean up in the **kitchen**. It was here that **Bruce** caught her trying to smuggle a dish of roast beef upstairs. Andi took the food up to the stray dog while the rest of the family was in the **den** watching TV. After searching the entire upstairs, they finally found the stray dog in the **sewing** closet. There Andi also found three brown-and-white **puppies**.

Chapter 4 *(Page 20)*
Vocabulary:

1. (e)   2. (h)   3. (a)   4. (j)   5. (b)   6. (i)   7. (c)   8. (d)   9. (f)   10. (g)

Questions:

1. Good – interesting; never boring; she never dragged.
   Bad – always shutting herself off someplace with her scribbling; bad temper; told lies.
2. *Answers may vary.* (i.e., find them a home; take them to the animal shelter)
3. Andi would stay home, pretending to be sick while she looked after the dogs, while Bruce went to school and tried to come up with a plan.
4. He made fun of his size saying he should be in kindergarten.
5. Seven.
6. The boy who had lived there had gotten into a run-in with Jerry and as a result none of the kids at school would have anything to do with him for fear of making Jerry mad.
7. He would rather be a loner and have no friends than hang around with someone like Jerry.
8. *Answers may vary.* (i.e. keep the stray dogs there).

Language Activities:

A. sale – school – seemed – setting – seventh – slowly – sometimes – standing – statement – surrounding
C. families – classes – puppies – districts – activities – hallways – bushes – choices – stomachaches – kindergartens

Research Activity:

New Mexico – about 521,999 – Rio Grande

Chapter 5 *(Page 24)*

Vocabulary:

1. decisive   2. bewildered   3. faucet   4. intent   5. tentative
6. cringe   7. interference 8. assault   9. adjust   10. appreciative

Questions:

1. Find homes for them.
2. *Answers may vary.*
3. a) Telling a lie.
   b) *Answers may vary* (i.e., he was honest; he didn't have much practice; he felt it was morally wrong to lie).
4. *Answers may vary.*
5. He was frightened and ran across the street where the wagon was hit by a car.
6. He was angry with Jerry and sided with Bruce.

Language Activity:

B. Just this past Tuesday, Jerry took Red Rover for a walk to Burger King.
   When did you get to see the Chicago Bulls play?
   Shania Twain was raised in the town of Timmins in northern Canada.

Chapter 6 *(Page 27)*

Vocabulary:

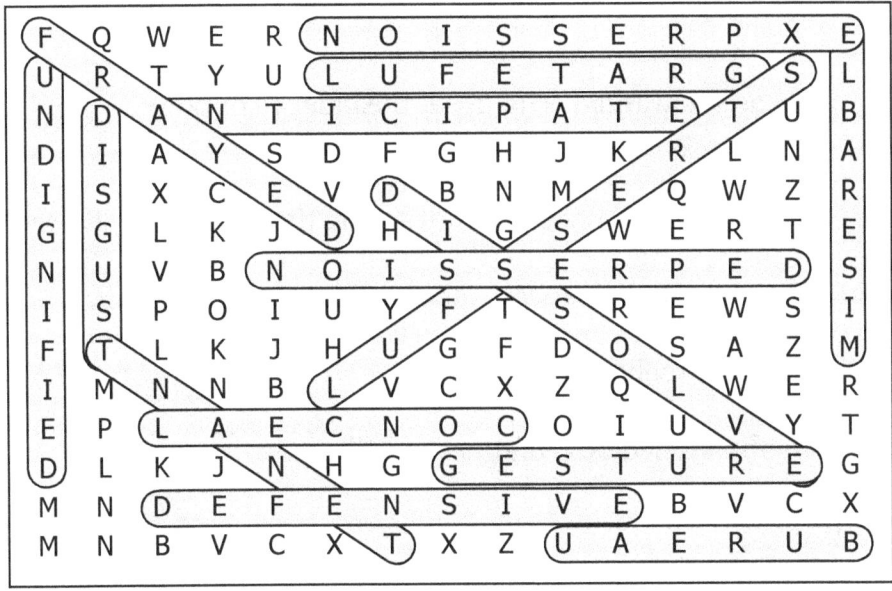

Questions:

1. In Elmwood, church and preparing for it consumed most of the day.
2. *Answers may vary.*
3. *Answers may vary.* (i.e., she was distracted by thinking of the puppies.)
4. It's because he lost something that belongs to him not because he loves Red Rover.
5. So she could sneak food for the dogs.
6. His hair was dull and lusterless, matted with mud and burrs. His tail was curled under him and his head was pressed against the ground. A frayed rope was around his neck.

7. Red Rover was going to stay in the vacant house.
8. *Answers may vary.* (i.e., He is a big dog that might not like being cooped up. They will have to feed him and exercise him.)

Chapter 7 *(Page 30)*

Vocabulary: *Answers may vary.*

Questions:
1. She accused him of being a spy and reporting back to Jerry because they were friends.
2. He would have Bruce for a friend.
3. So Jerry wouldn't see them carrying the boards across to the vacant house.
4. *Answers may vary.* (i.e., they were guests in Aunt Alice's home).
5. *Answers may vary.*
6. *Answers may vary.* (i.e., She has company and may not be as lonely. She must find it difficult having so many people living with her when she is used to living by herself).
7. *Answers may vary.*

A. 1. furious   2. rinse   3. comfort   4. active   5. certain
    6. decide   7. transform   8. responsible

Chapter 8 *(Page 34)*

Vocabulary:
1. resent   2. irritable   3. infuriated   4. picky   5. inconceivable
6. goriest 7. admiration 8. solemn   9. ungracious 10. visualized

Questions:
1. Andi wasn't able to run things exactly as she wanted. Tim upset the balance of power.
2. Dog food, brush and comb, salve.
3. *Answers may vary.*
4. At the bottom of the form there was a handwritten note to Andi saying that her poem showed promise.
5. Helicopter pilot – she was afraid of heights. Ballet dancer – she wasn't graceful enough. A teacher – not enough patience.
6. Her friends and her brother thought only dweebs wrote poetry.
7. *Answers may vary.*
8. Debbie told her about MacTavish, an abandoned dog, that needed a home.

Chapter 9 *(Page 37)*

Vocabulary:
1. (b) 2. (d) 3. (a) 4. (b) 5. (c) 6. (a) 7. (d) 8. (c) 9. (a) 10. (c)

1. He was delighted.
2. They were already working very hard to buy food for the dogs they had and didn't know how they would be able to keep the dogs fed.
3. He was upset at his low grades.
4. The alarm woke up everybody in the house.
5. He wasn't getting enough sleep and was tired all day.
6. *Answers may vary.* (i.e., A fog made it appear earlier than it really was, so when he took

Red Rover for a walk, the dog got away. The paper boy saw him and suggested to Bruce that it was Jerry's dog and he was going to notify Jerry.)
7. *Answers may vary.* (i.e., to provide excitement for the reader.)

Language Activities:
C. Compound Words: ourselves, anything, housework, afternoon, outdoor, playtime, sometimes, doorbell, upstairs, eyelids

Chapter 10 *(Page 41)*

Vocabulary:
1. forlorn - cheerful
2. reasonable - absurd
3. absolute - limited
4. enthusiastic - apathetic
5. exotic - plain
6. delight - dismay
7. permission - prohibition

1. permission 2. absolute 3. reasonable 4. forlorn 5. enthusiastic
6. exotic 7. delight

Questions:
1. True 2. False 3. True 4. False 5. True 6. False 7. True
8. True 9. False 10. True

Chapter 11 *(Page 44)*

Vocabulary:
1. protective 2. skeptical 3. intently 4. frantic 5. torture
6. triumphant 7. irritable 8. determination 9. confident 10. disbelief

Questions:
1. He didn't look nearly as imposing when he was alone.
2. She almost revealed to Jerry that she knew too much about Red Rover's condition and whereabouts since his disappearance.
3. Red Rover's ghost.
4. Jerry believes in ghosts.
5. She would write poems for presents and sew things like pincushions and neckties.
6. a) They take dogs in as boarders.
   b) *Answers may vary.*

Chapter 12 *(Page 47)*

Vocabulary:
1. obvious 2. prelude 3. accommodations 4. insist 5. regretful
6. impression 7. astonishment 8. alterations 9. intently 10. desperately

Questions:
1. a) A beagle.
   b) He was a lively dog and strong for his size.
2. The owners were once again living in the house.
3. a) She was distressed.
   b) Andi thought Aunt Alice would be happy to see them go.
4. a) He howled very loudly, so the whole neighborhood heard him. It would alert the neighbors to the fact that there were dogs in the vacant house.

b) She said it was Red Rover's ghost howling for revenge. *Answers may vary.*

Chapter 13 *(Page 50)*

Vocabulary: *Answers may vary.*

Questions:
1. *Answers may vary.* (i.e., Midnight is a spooky time. The adults will all be asleep.)
2. a) adobe – a sun-dried brick made of clay and straw
   b) tumbleweeds – a plant like the Russian thistle uprooted and driven about by the wind
   c) arroyos - a small steep-sided watercourse or gulch with a nearly flat floor: usually dry except after heavy rains
   d) aspens – a type of poplar tree
3. The picture of her dog, Bebe.
4. Debbie.
5. They used the projector to shine a picture of Red Rover through his bedroom window and onto the wall while Andi howled outside the window.
6. Jerry's parents woke up and caused a commotion. Bruce and the others panicked and ran off without unplugging the projector. This caused the cord to be ripped from the projector which they left on the ground attached to the extension cord.

Chapter 14 *(Page 53)*

Vocabulary: 1. queasy 2. confident 3. depressed 4. grim 5. traditional 6. precise 7. convenient 8. bewilder 9. melodious 10. wretched

Questions:
1. *Answers may vary.* (i.e., They were expecting Jerry's dad to come over and get them in trouble for what they did to Jerry.)
2. The evidence they left behind (extension cord, cord from the projector).
3. He was the real estate agent who was helping Andi's parents find a house to live in.
4. The vacant house down the street where the dogs were staying.
5. *Answers may vary.* (i.e., They discovered the dogs staying there and Andi and Bruce had to explain what they were up to.)
6. Call the pound.
7. They saw Jerry, his dad, and Red Rover approaching them along the sidewalk.

Chapter 15 *(Page 56)*

Vocabulary: 1. (b) 2. (d) 3. (a) 4. (c) 5. (a) 6. (d) 7. (b) 8. (c)

Questions:
1. He was angry with Jerry and asked why no one had told him.
2. a) He felt they should be arrested for break and entry.
   b) Aunt Alice defended the children and Andi's parents decided to buy the house.
3. Her late husband had been a detective and she had helped him in his business.
4. He said that Bruce could pay for Red Rover over time. He felt that Jerry wasn't responsible enough to own a dog.
5. *Answers may vary.* (i.e., when Bruce was given Red Rover).
6. *Answers may vary.*

www.ingramcontent.com/pod-product-compliance
Lightning Source LLC
Chambersburg PA
CBHW050351100426
42734CB00041B/3143